GET OUT ALIVE!

ESCAPE FROM RAZOR TEETH

Julie K. Lundgren

Published in the United States of America by Cherry Lake Publishing Group
Ann Arbor, Michigan
www.cherrylakepublishing.com

Reading Adviser: Beth Walker Gambro, MS, Ed., Reading Consultant, Yorkville, IL

Photo Credits:
© Martin Kominko/Shutterstock, cover (coati), page 23 (top), Colin Eaton/Shutterstock cover (spider), page 20 (top), © klyaksun/Shutterstock (graphic on cover and throughout book); © Cassette Bleue/Shutterstock, speech bubbles throughout; © Nazarkru/Shutterstock, yellow bursts throughout; © Kokhanchikov/Shutterstock page 4, map © ArtMari/Shutterstock; © Zhanrui Ye/Shutterstock (top), © Danny Ye/Shutterstock page 5; © Dmitri Gomon/Shutterstock page 6; © 1630131286/Shutterstock page 7; © Lubos Chlubny/ Shutterstock (top), © Stefan Lambauer/Shutterstock page 8; © Natalia Golovina/Shutterstock (top), © Filippo Carlot/Shutterstock page 9; © PetlinDmitry/Shutterstock page 10; © guentermanaus/Shutterstock page 11(top), page 12 (bottom), © Milan Zygmunt/Shutterstock page 11 (bottom), page 12 (top), page 13, page 15; © Matt Gush/Shutterstock page 14; © Dan Olsen/Shutterstock page 16 (top), © Rob Jansen/Shutterstock page 16 (bottom); © IH82/Shutterstock page 17; © Audrey Snider-Bell/Shutterstock page 18 and 22; © Skatwix/Shutterstock page 19; © Tobias Hauke/Shutterstock page 20; © ChandelleB/Shutterstock page 21; © Pandora Pictures/Shutterstock page 23 (bottom).

Produced for Cherry Lake Publishing by bluedooreducation.com

Copyright © 2026 by Cherry Lake Publishing Group

All rights reserved. No part of this book may be reproduced or utilized in any form or by any means without written permission from the publisher.

Library of Congress Cataloging-in-Publication Data has been filed and is available at catalog.loc.gov.

Printed in the United States of America

Note from Publisher: Websites change regularly, and their future contents are outside of our control. Supervise children when conducting any recommended online searches for extended learning opportunities.

About the Author

Julie K. Lundgren grew up in northern Minnesota near Lake Superior. She delighted in picking berries, finding cool rocks, and trekking in the woods. She still does! Julie's interest in nature science led her to a degree in biology. She adores her family, her sweet cat, and Adventure Days.

Contents

COATI CRUNCH 4
A MIGHTY SPIDER 10
THE SNACK THAT
FIGHTS BACK! 14
FIND OUT MORE 24
GLOSSARY 24
INDEX 24

SOUTH AMERICAN COATIS LIVE IN THE FORESTS OF NORTHERN SOUTH AMERICA. THEY USE THEIR TAILS FOR BALANCE WHEN THEY CLIMB THROUGH THE TREES.

Coatis are quick and clever. They climb well like monkeys and lemurs. They have banded tails like raccoons.

COATIS EAT WHATEVER THEY CAN CATCH, DIG OUT, OR SNAP UP. THEY USE THEIR CLAWS TO DIG UNDER ROOTS AND IN BURROWS. THEY EAT:

- BIRD EGGS
- INSECTS
- CENTIPEDES
- MILLIPEDES
- SPIDERS
- LIZARDS
- FRUIT

Coatis are deadly hunters. Check out these razor-sharp teeth. They slice and crunch!

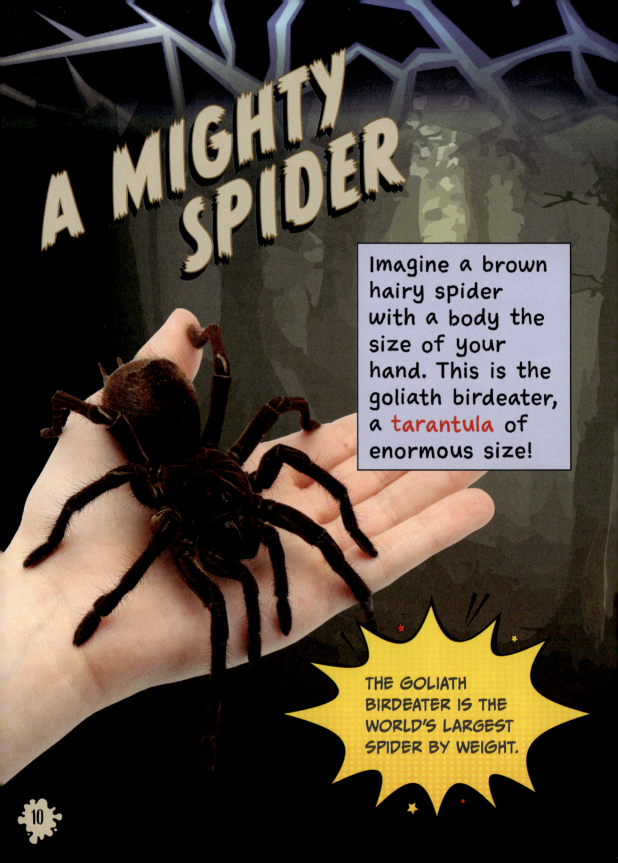

A MIGHTY SPIDER

Imagine a brown hairy spider with a body the size of your hand. This is the goliath birdeater, a *tarantula* of enormous size!

THE GOLIATH BIRDEATER IS THE WORLD'S LARGEST SPIDER BY WEIGHT.

By day, goliath birdeaters rest in burrows under tree roots and rocks. At night, they hunt on the tropical rainforest floor.

I don't hunt birds much. Instead, I eat insects, mice, and frogs.

Hairs on the tarantula's legs and body sense when prey is moving nearby.

Goliath birdeaters do not catch prey in webs. They use their fangs to inject prey with venom. The venom turns the prey's insides to liquid. The spider sucks the prey dry.

Goliath birdeaters have a hard shell, or carapace. They molt this carapace many times in their lives. Shedding the carapace lets them grow a bit bigger before the new shell hardens.

HISSSSSS!

GOLIATH BIRDEATERS RUB THEIR HAIRY LEGS TOGETHER TO MAKE A HISSING SOUND. THIS WARNS PREDATORS TO STAY AWAY.

THE SNACK THAT FIGHTS BACK!

COATIS HOLD THEIR TAILS UP AS THEY HUNT FOR FOOD.

Deep in the tropical forest, a young coati searches for food. It flips over leaves and opens rotting logs. It looks for insects and other tasty snacks.

A goliath birdeater female comes out of her burrow. Her huge size means she has molted many times in her life.

GOLIATH BIRDEATERS MOLT 5 OR 6 TIMES IN THEIR FIRST YEAR.

The tarantula senses footsteps coming closer. She steps into a shadow. She stands very still.

The coati is close! The goliath birdeater bares her fangs. She makes a scritchy hissing sound. Back away, coati!

WARNING!

GOLIATH BIRDEATERS RAISE THEIR FRONT LEGS TO SHOW THEIR FANGS.

The coati ignores both warnings. It comes closer. It has seen other coati eat these leggy beasts.

THE COATI SEES THE SPIDER AS A LARGE, CRUNCHY SNACK.

The coati tries to grab the giant spider. It wants to drag it across the ground to break off the spiky hairs.

The goliath birdeater unleashes her secret weapon. She flings her barbed hairs at the coati. The hairs stick in its face like tiny darts.

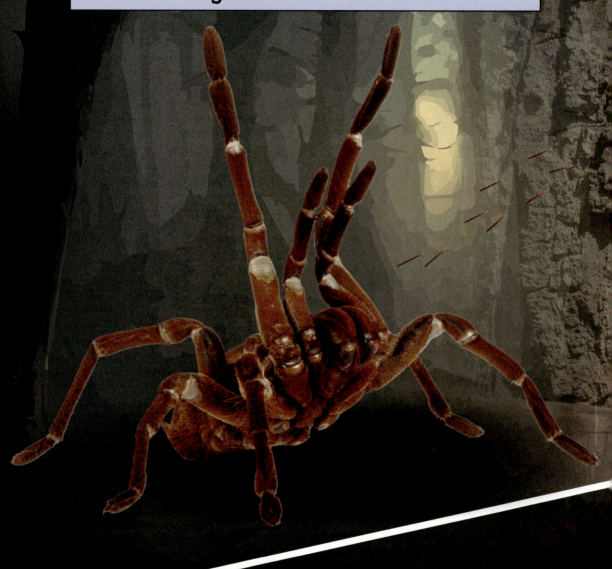

Find Out More

Books

Markovics, Joyce. *White-nosed Coati*, Minneapolis, MN: Bearport, 2013

Archer, Claire. *Tarantula Spiders*, Minneapolis, MN: Abdo Kids, 2015

Websites

Search these online sources with an adult:

Coatis | National Geographic Kids
Goliath birdeater | San Diego Zoo

Glossary

barbs (BARBZ) small, sharp spikes used for defense

carapace (KAIR-uh-payce) the hard shell of an insect or spider

carnivores (KAR-nuh-vorz) hunter animals with teeth adapted to eating meat

coati (KWAH-tee) a forest dweller that is related to raccoons

flexible (FLEKS-uh-bull) able to move freely in many directions

molt (MOHLT) shed a hard outer body shell in order to grow

predators (PRED-uh-turz) animals hunted and eaten by other animals

prey (PRAY) animals hunted and eaten by other animals

tarantula (tuh-RAN-chuh-luh) large, hairy spider living in North and South America

venom (VEH-num) a poison made by some animals like snakes and spiders to kill prey

Index

burrow(s) 7, 11, 15
carapace 13
fangs 12, 13, 18
hairs 11, 13, 17, 20, 21, 22, 23
hiss(ing) 13, 18
molt(ed) 13, 15
prey 11, 12
snout(s) 6
tail(s) 4, 5, 14, 17
teeth 8, 9
venom 12
weapon 13, 22